The Amazing Adventures of
Oliver Hill

Seventeen Short Stories based on
Napoleon Hill's **Principles of Success**.

by Havilah Malone and Diane Lampe
with Illustrations by Youjin Oh

An official publication of
THE NAPOLEON HILL FOUNDATION

Published by:

> The Napoleon Hill Foundation
> P.O. Box 1277
> Wise, Virginia USA 24293
> Website: www.naphill.org
> Email: napoleonhill@uvawise.edu

> Napoleon Hill World Learning Center
> Purdue University Calumet
> 2300 173rd Street
> Hammond, Indiana 46323
> Email: nhf@purduecal.edu

THE AMAZING ADVENTURES OF OLIVER HILL

ISBN: 978-1-942491-01-9

FOREWORD

Dear Parents, Relatives, Teachers, Mentors, and Friends,

Other than food, shelter, and clothing, reading is the very next best thing that you can do for your children to prepare them for their future. Not only does reading enrich the mind but it helps young personalities grow and bloom into a sense of purpose with an understanding of what life is about.

Readers are truly leaders in all walks of life, and the gift of reading is a legacy for a lifetime. How do I know this? I am certain of these facts by the way my mother cultivated reading in my development and gave me the gift of having an infinite number of teachers in books and stories. I was not place bound because of where I lived. From my early years I traveled and learned about new people, countries, and cultures through books. I read biographies, learned about saints and sinners, and enjoyed silly stories as one of my favorite pastimes through reading.

I read out loud, to my mother, to my dolls, and even to my cats if they were a willing audience. But in fact, all the time, I was reading to and for myself. Today, I am certified as a reading professional K-12 and hold a license to develop a school reading program that advances through the grade levels. I can also work to diagnose reading problems in individuals. But, that is not what I choose to do now. Instead, I choose to instill the value of reading in people through my authorship of writings aligned with Napoleon Hill's works.

I see a void between young people of today and those from decades ago. Reading needs to be introduced and "massaged" into our children so that they will know where to turn for help and feel good about the process. Scientists, psychologists, and every reader knows the intrinsic value of reading in introducing children to life's values and beliefs that help sustain them into adulthood and even old age.

Reading is an elixir, a fountain of youth, a trophy that is a passageway to the very best future that you can gift a child. But, the books read need to be quality readings. They need to inspire mind work like imagination, creativity, dedication, discipline, and self-care that will create pathways in the brain that exceed what happens without reading.

In a study of elderly nuns' ongoing brain capacity, it was recently found that those nuns who read from an early age were less inclined to display symptoms of Alzheimer's disease in their senior years, even if they were genetically predisposed and were expected to display the symptoms. Why? Because through reading, new neurological pathways were created early on in the brain that gave them alternative methods to think and respond when old pathways were mangled or destroyed.

In the book entitled *Aging With Grace* that shares findings from the Nun Study, author David Snowdon, Ph.D. quotes Dr. Susan Kemper, a psycholinguist who studies the impact of aging on language skills. Dr. Kemper states adamantly that "the best way to increase vocabulary and reading comprehension is by starting early in life, by reading to your children." This one action, reading to children, is powerful and can increase the brain's growth and activity throughout a person's lifetime. The simple answer unequivocally is to read to children which in turn aids in the creation of multiple connections between nerve cells. This simple activity works to enhance our brain capacity.

Reading is like brain insurance. Reading is like the magical potion that can assist us in sustaining our brain functions well into our 80's and 90's. Remember this significant fact. This only works if children have been read to and became readers themselves at an early age. Truly, reading widens our horizons and cultivates texture and richness in our daily lives and later experiences as an adult.

By beginning with this book of examples and suggestions, you can introduce your child to reading for pleasure and purpose. If at first you express joy in reading, and model this behavior often at home your child will too. By reading daily you catch the attention of your child at a young age and they imprint your behavior and want to do what you are doing. Reading is contagious and something very good to catch. No vaccine required.

Reading suggestions in this book are my personal choices and examples. They correspond to the principles that Dr. Napoleon Hill teaches for a lifetime of richness and success in many ways. If you go to the library, purchase a book, read it online, or find it elsewhere, you will benefit your children immensely.

By reading the children's rhymed stories written by Havilah Malone and Diane Lampe, you will be giving your child an appetizer that encourages them to find hidden nutrition in stories that can feed them for life. All it takes is a little effort on your part, or the part of a relative or mentor, who wants to introduce children to the joys and benefits of reading. Whether you read for fun, for education, for armchair traveling, for a release from the ordinary, or to cultivate your imagination and creativity, to learn how people lived astounding lives, or just to pass time, reading contains something for everyone.

Reading is a gift that literally lasts a lifetime, keeps on giving, and grows a brain full of beauty and richness. Particulars aside, reading is a fun and valuable activity that allows each and every one of us to become the person we envision becoming.

Fail to read. Fail to succeed. It is as simple and complex as that. Readers are leaders. If you want to be one, get out those books and learn the lessons of your choice.

Happy Reading!
Be Your Very Best Always through READING!
Judith Williamson

INTRODUCTION

Whatever the mind can conceive
and believe, the mind can achieve.
                        —NAPOLEON HILL

Welcome to an Amazing Adventure you will not soon forget
of Oliver, Olivia, and Big Zeke who you've not yet met.
You'll also meet their friends, who are very much like you,
enjoying life and every day learning something new.
These lessons from Dr. Hill will guide you your whole life through
into a wonderful world of possibilities that you never knew.
As you read these amazing adventures keep an open mind,
deep inside lie hidden treasures that you are sure to find.
Let the journey begin as you Make Your Dreams Come True.

All the Best,
Happy Wishes to You!
Havilah & Diane

THE AMAZING LEMONADE STAND

#1 Definiteness of Purpose

It was another sunny day,
and Oliver was dreaming away.
How could he get his brother and sister
to come out and play?

Olivia was always busy
laughing with her friends.
In her own small world playing pretend.

His older brother Big Zeke
had his head stuck in a book.
Oliver pleaded, "Look, Big Zeke look...
those books can wait another day.
Please come out and play!"

Big Zeke shook his head, "not today,"
and Olivia just laughed him away.

Oliver with head hanging low for all to see,
went and sat by his favorite lemon tree.
Deciding that he would find a way
to get Big Zeke and Olivia to come out and play!

His little puppy Cody mischievous as could be,
grabbed a lemon from the lemon tree.

He brought it to Oliver, but wouldn't let it go.
Oliver stood up and shouted, "Now I know!
A lemonade stand is what it will be
for Big Zeke, Olivia, and me!"

With Mom and Dad's help, work was under way
and Oliver's excitement and giggling
could be heard throughout the day.

Big Zeke began to peek from behind his book,
and Olivia's curiosity brought her outside to look.
Neither could believe what they saw with their eyes,
the amazing family lemonade stand. What a big surprise!

Big Zeke and Olivia asked Oliver,
"Can we come over and play?"
"Of course," Oliver replied,
"that would make my day!"

Oliver was so excited
that his dream had come true
of getting his big brother and sister
to play with him as he knew he could do.

THE ICE CREAM CONTEST
#2 Mastermind Alliance

It was that special time of year,
when the county fair hit high gear.
People came from everywhere
to compete in contests at the fair.

Oliver wanted to find something he could do
to participate in the contests too.
When he looked down the list to his surprise,
an ice cream flavor contest caught his eye.

He thought what a fun contest that would be,
to create a yummy flavor and win easily.
And getting to eat ice cream all day
wasn't such a bad price to pay.

The milk from his cow was of the highest grade
and would create the best ice cream ever made.

He knew he couldn't do it alone
so he decided to pick up the phone.
Oliver thought to himself, "Who will I call
that can make a flavor that would be pleasing to all?"

"Julie, Julie that's who,
she makes the best sweets. I love them. Don't you?"
He asked Julie to come and she readily agreed,
"A new ice cream flavor, that's brilliant indeed!"

"Wait there's more," Oliver chimed in,
"we still need a helping hand to ensure our win.
Who came to mind, well wouldn't you know...
It was our friend and good neighbor, Joe!"

He had the strength to churn ice cream all day.
Just add sugar and cream and the best milk in town,
and with Julie's flavor they'll win best all around.

The work began and the fun did too,
eating lots of ice cream was a dream come true.
When the flavor hit their tummies, everyone agreed
it would be the winner guaranteed.
Now came the day the country fair had arrived.
"We were ready. Julie, Joe, and I."

"As the judges tasted all the flavors
    that were there,
we were right, our ice cream was
    beyond compare.
We won the trophy and took
    first prize,
doing it together, Julie, Joe, and I."

THE BIGGEST SPLASH
#3 Applied Faith

Another summer was to come and pass
without Oliver experiencing a splash.
Since no one ever taught him how to swim,
his fear grew bigger and bigger and overcame him.

He watched all his friends and it made him sore,
as they jumped in and splashed and made quite a roar.
His secret desire was to learn how to swim,
but he was afraid his friends would make fun of him.

It was the hottest day of the year
and again Oliver was full of fear.
He avoided the water the best he could,
but no one really understood.

His teacher Mrs. Judy saw the fright on
   his face.
She was confused, that look was so
   out of place.
"Oliver, my dear, tell me what's wrong?"

Ashamed and embarrassed, Oliver
   quietly said,
"I don't know how to swim, so I stand
   here instead.
My friends will laugh because I don't,
so I never tried, and I won't."

With a warm smile Mrs. Judy lovingly said,
"You can do it if you believe you can.
I will teach you, just take my hand."

Mrs. Judy began giving lessons to him.
He learned how to float,
even backstroke and swim.

Oliver's confidence grew very strong
because he took action to move it along.

Summer was leaving with haste
and there was no time to waste.

Oliver ran to the great swimming hole
to finally accomplish a lifelong goal.
Jumping right in for the biggest splash of the year,
once and for all getting rid of his fear!

MEATLOAF MONDAY
#4 Going the Extra Mile

Monday is this family's favorite day of the week.
Ready to eat, the kids head off to seek
the delicious food prepared by their Mother.
She makes a mean meatloaf like no other.

What sets it apart from all of the rest
are the freshest ingredients
    that have passed the test.

Each of the children has a part to play
in gathering fresh farm food
    for Meatloaf Monday.

The journey begins to find the best of the best
as Big Zeke, Olivia and Oliver set out for the quest.

As they approach the tall tomato vine,
Big Zeke grabbed a ladder and started to climb.
Olivia said, "not that one, go to the top,
only the juiciest from this crop."

Now that Big Zeke's sack is full off they all go
to find the next ingredient in Mom's meatloaf.

Oliver said, "Let's protect our eyes,
because strong onions can make you cry."
So out came the goggles from Oliver's sack,
Big Zeke and Olivia were happy he made the pack.

With a pep in their step and singing a song,
they went down each row and gathered along,
not the bruised ones or brown ones or ones with holes,
only firm onions in their sacks could meet their goals.

Even though the kids' tummies began to growl
it would not stop them from going the extra mile.

As they passed the garlic, Olivia grabbed a couple of cloves,
now to the chicken coop they had to go past the groves.

Yippee, one more ingredient to place in their sacks
was the farm fresh eggs so they would not crack.

Now that their quest is finally complete,
They pick up their sacks and head home
        to eat.

Mom and Dad met them at the door with
        a smile,
"We're proud of you for going the extra
        mile."

When the family sat down to eat,
all agreed this was the Meatloaf Monday
        to beat!
It was far superior than all of the rest.
This Meatloaf Monday more than
        passed the test.

YOU MAKE ME SMILE
#5 Pleasing Personality

When Olivia walks into a room
with a big smile on her face,
her energy is felt all over the place.

Olivia shines a light wherever she goes.
Her light comes from inside, everyone knows.

To this fact, her teachers can attest
Olivia always tries to do her very best.

She's cooperative and respectful
and strives for success.
And works really hard to do well on
    her tests.

Olivia may struggle a time or two
learning something new as most
    people do
but she'll find a way to see it through.

Even when change isn't easy to embrace,
she keeps a positive expression on her face.

As she gets on the bus at the end of the day,
Olivia sees her brother who had nothing to say.

He was looking out the window at a sky so grey.
Feeling sad and alone, wanting it to go away.

She sits next to him wearing a big grin,
"Oliver, whatever it is will go away,
I'm here for you if you want me to stay."

Oliver quickly replied, "Of course I do,
I already feel better because of you."

Olivia then shared, "Whenever I feel down
a big smile always helps to turn it around.
I instantly feel better inside and out,
when a kind word is spoken when I'm in doubt."

Olivia's big smile makes people feel good.
She has a big smile as everyone should.

CAMP FIRE FUN
#6 Personal Initiative

The packing and planning was done,
now the boys were headed to Camp Fire Fun.

Camp Counselor Brown said with delight,
"To make this trip easy from the start,
each of us must play our part."

"How good you do is up to you,
we'll see how well you follow through.
Here's your assignments so gather round,
no cutting corners or trashing camp ground."

"Neil and Will – gather wood and make a big pile,
the bigger the pile the bigger my smile."

As the rest of the assignments were handed out,
all of the boys began to shout,
"We're so happy we are going to see a bear,
roast marshmallows and tell stories that
    scare."

Off into the woods the boys began to
    go.
When Neil and Will came back
    wouldn't you know...
Neil's wood pile was so very low.

He only brought back four pieces, no, it was three...
a pile so low, as low as could be.

Next came Will, who always went the extra mile
and what do you know, he had a really big pile!

He brought back not eight...not even nine,
but came back to camp with twenty-four in a line.

Neil cornered Will and sarcastically said,
"Why did you bring back that much wood,
it makes it look like I did less than I should?"

Will replied with confidence in his voice,
"I did it because it was the right choice.
We'll have a big fire when all the work is done.
You should try it; you'll have so much more fun."

Neil thought about why he didn't try harder,
just trying to get by shows he's not a self-starter.
He wanted to change and change he would,
by doing it again the very best he could.

Into the woods Neil went at a quick pace,
with a new found attitude seen on his face.
He brought back such a humongous pile
that Camp Counselor Brown had to smile.

In the dark of night the fire blazed bright
and all the boys cheered in sheer delight.
They agreed this trip was #1,
truly unforgettable Camp Fire Fun!

OLIVIA'S NEW BIKE
#7 Positive Mental Attitude

One of the best events of the year
is the school bike race that was
    drawing near.

Olivia wanted to enter the race
so she could win and take first place.

The problem was she didn't have a bike
or the money to buy one that she
    would like.

So she decided to ask her mom for the
    money.
Her mom replied, "Sorry, we don't
    have it, Honey."

"There's a bike in the garage, covered
    with dust
you know the one...that is all full of rust?
It needs new parts and a little work too,
but that could be the solution for you."

Olivia excitedly said, "Mom, what a
    wonderful idea!
With my brothers' help, we could find the
    right parts.
There's no way I could lose...I'm ready to start!"

Her brothers agreed and off they all went,
looking for parts that wouldn't cost a cent.

They gathered two tires, brakes and pedals,
shiny used parts that were all full of metal.
They found handle bars and a comfy seat too
and a strong chain link that looked brand new.

Olivia was overjoyed they found what they needed.
In their search for the right parts they truly succeeded.

Today the school race was finally here.
Friends and family were lined up to cheer.

In the beginning Olivia took off at a very fast pace,
but she never practiced and was all over the place.

After crossing the finish line she jumped up and down.
Although everyone was surely expecting a frown.

With a confused look on the crowd's face,
her brothers blurted out, "You didn't win the race!"

With a beaming smile Olivia cheerfully replied,
"I know I didn't win but I still had so much fun
even without winning I still feel like number one.
Spending time together building this bike with you
was so much better than buying one brand new."

"Now I can practice and prepare for the race,
with your help next year I will take first place!"

THE TOWN OF LOST AND FOUND

#8 Enthusiasm

Fear and famine filled the *Town of Lost and Found,*
wherever you looked no food was around.

The farmer's son Oliver saw his mother in tears.
He wanted to fix it and get rid of her fears.

Remembering his grandfather's story
about a seed that grows when fed,
not with water but *LOVE* instead.

He dug out the seeds from a secret chest.
Excited and ready to save his town,
Oliver ran screaming and shouting,
"Look what I found!"

The people scoffed and laughed
and shooed him away.

The young man Oliver decided,
I'll Do It Anyway!
"If It's To Be, It's Up To Me,"
said Oliver enthusiastically.

In a hurry he ran home as fast as he could,
knowing that he could do so much good.

Holding each seed in his hand, eyes closed tight,
he sang this song with all his might,
"Oh seed, oh seed I am grateful to thee,
I give you all the love I have within me."

That night as he laid his head upon his bed,
his burning desire was for his town to be fed.

By morning the seeds started to sprout.
As the postman passed by he began to shout,
"Look, I can't believe they are really out!"

Oliver exclaimed,
"More love, more love is what we need
to make them grow faster indeed."

The postman then spread the word from
    house to house,
"The more love you give, the more the
    seeds will sprout."

Oliver went on to save the town...
they were no longer lost but finally found.

THE BIG SPELLING BEE
#9 Self-Discipline

Whenever you see Big Zeke
you'll only catch a glimpse of his eyes.
His head will be in a book,
to his friends that's no surprise.

Last week he brought home a trophy
for winning the Big Spelling Bee.
This was no small feat, as you will soon see.

At school, Mr. Martinez had news to share
and his excitement was without compare.

"We are going to the Regional Spelling Bee.
Big Zeke you are the one chosen to compete."

With a stunned and terrified look in
    his eyes,
Big Zeke found this news a very big
    surprise!

Mr. Martinez continued...
"We know you'll be the one, all your classmates agree,
you'll bring home the trophy and win the spelling bee."

"Our school has never won although we've tried and tried."
All the kids began to cheer to show they were on his side.

Big Zeke felt overwhelmed and didn't know what to say.
He thought about it but the fear simply wouldn't go away.

"I can do this, I'll practice night and day
and I won't let anything get in my way."

Although his friends would stop by
to ask Big Zeke to come out and play
he would say, "No thanks, not today."

He continued to study and practice,
with his head stuck in a book.
Determined to do whatever it took!

As the Regional Spelling Bee began,
everything went according to plan.

At first Big Zeke easily won round after round,
as his class cheered him on with a thunderous sound.

The words got harder as the day moved along,
and then his fear of losing became very strong.
This was a feeling he knew he could not allow,
as the sweat started to drip down from his brow.

The last word was announced
and it was a difficult word indeed
but all of Big Zeke's work paid off
with a Spelling Bee Victory.

He took home the trophy and brought his school a win.
The word he spelled correctly was "Self-Discipline."

NO FISH TODAY
#10 Accurate Thinking

When the school bell rang at the end of the day,
Oliver watched as the older boys passed his way.

As usual they were heading to their fishing spot,
all the way at the end of the abandoned lot.

The lot was dense and full of trees.
You couldn't even see beyond the leaves.
Oliver wondered what they *really* did out there.

"We are going fishing," the older boys would say,
but no poles or fish were seen day after day.

Kids looking on let their imaginations take flight
and instantly replied with their own insight.

"They go into the woods to set large fires.
No matter what they say, they're all big liars.
They sneak into coops and steal chicken eggs.
They even capture frogs and bite off their legs."

Oliver said, "No that can't be,
I'll find out for myself just wait and see."

Oliver followed the boys the very next day
making sure he stayed far, far away.

He watched them go through the dense trees,
in some spots even crawling on their knees.

It was hard to keep up but Oliver wanted to know.
As the journey went on his curiosity started to grow.

They reached a clearing at the end of the lot,
finally arriving at their fishing spot.

Much to Oliver's surprise
there were the poles waiting inside
a small boat the boys called 'Pride.'

Oliver was happy when he saw what came next,
they released each fish they caught in their net.

He watched as the boys laughed and had fun
and couldn't wait to tell everyone...

Sometimes things aren't what they seem.
These boys were fishing,
fishing indeed!

THE MUSIC IN ME
#11 Controlled Attention

Olivia's class was going to see a Special Musical Play
but she had little to no interest in going that day.

The musical began and she couldn't have been more wrong,
she was standing and clapping and singing along.

That night Olivia lost sleep tossing and turning in bed,
she simply couldn't get the music out of her head.

Morning came and she couldn't wait to get to school
to speak to her Band Director Mrs. O'Toole.

Olivia talked on and on about the Special Musical Play
and how her greatest desire was to have a solo one day.

"It'll take hard work I already know
but I really want my very own Solo."

"I'll make the commitment and stop playing around
once I get focused I'll create the best sound."

Mrs. O'Toole replied with glee,
"I'm glad you are finally taking it more seriously.
I've always known the clarinet was perfect for you,
now apply yourself and show me what you can do."

Olivia happily brought home her clarinet
to learn a lesson she would not soon forget.

She pulled it out excited to play a musical tune
but to her surprise it wouldn't happen too soon.
She realized she needed to learn the notes.
Especially how to hold the clarinet right,
and this certainly would not happen overnight.

Olivia continued to practice day after day,
knowing hard work and dedication bring a solo her way.

The night of the school play had finally arrived
and Olivia's level of practice could not be denied.
She took center stage and played with all her might
as everyone clapped and cheered in sheer delight!

Her heart's desire to play had finally come true
and you can find the music in you!

TEA PARTY MADNESS
#12 Teamwork

Olivia was sitting in her room one day
remembering the tradition her Grandma passed her way.

Throwing Tea Parties made Grandma DeDe the talk of the town
bringing people together from all around.

To have an experience like no other
and Olivia wanted to be just like her grandmother.

Continuing this tradition and showing her friends something new,
Olivia decided she wanted to throw a Tea Party too.

"Elegance and glitz is what it will be.
Mother can I please throw a Tea Party?"
"That would be wonderful!" her mother agreed.

"Mom I'm so excited to work as a team
to turn this into my Tea Party Dream!

I'll invite Annabel, Kayla and Juliet too.
Monet, Mia, and Mya and the Malone twins,
    just to name a few."

Baking for the big day began
as Olivia and her Mother worked their Tea Party plan.

With their hands covered in batter and dough,
the amount of cookies started to grow.

Olivia and her mother cheerfully sang,
when the front doorbell suddenly rang.

As they both turned around without missing a beat,
their little dog Cody snuck in for a treat.

He jumped on the counter and made quite a mess,
turning her Tea Party Dream into Tea Party Madness.

His paw hit the pan and dough flew in the air
and teacups came crashing down everywhere.

Olivia turned back and let out an enormous scream,
"PLEASE STOP HIM Mother, he's ruining everything!"

There was a big sticky mess on the floor
as her friend Kayla walked through the door.

"Don't worry my dear we'll put Cody outside
and we'll get everything together," her mother calmly replied.

Kayla chimed in, "I will help you too,
that is what a good friend would do."

They cleaned up the mess as quick as could be
and continued to prepare for the Tea Party.

Sandwiches were cut into small bites
as they baked up new cookie delights.

The house filled with the smell of fresh brewed tea
as her friends started arriving for the Tea Party.

Mother, Olivia and Kayla made a great team,
turning Tea Party Madness into a Tea Party Dream.

FROM ASHES
TO BLACK GOLD
#13 Learning From Adversity & Defeat

Oliver, Olivia and Big Zeke were getting off the bus
as Mother sat quietly waiting with news to discuss.

They walked to the door and stopped at the steps.
Something bad happened and it was quite complex.
Mother sadly shared, "Our biggest fear has come true
and your father and I are deciding what to do."

"One thing after another has not gone our way
now the family barn burned to the ground today.
But you don't have to worry the animals are okay."

"So much has gone wrong since we moved to this town,
it's time to pick up and find some new ground."

The kids were in disbelief from what they heard
and the thought of leaving was truly absurd.

Olivia pleaded, "You taught us not to run away
even when things aren't going our way.
We can make it through even though it's bad.
Please don't make us leave, let's talk to dad."

Oliver and Big Zeke eagerly agreed too,
they needed a better plan for what to do.

"We don't even mind selling all of our toys,
we'd rather stay here, it would bring us more joy.
All of our friends at our school will help too.
Let's rebuild the barn and start anew."

Overwhelmed by the kids response that day,
it touched Mother's heart in a positive way.
So she talked to their dad and decided to stay.

Mother reached out to her book club friends,
while neighboring farmers began pitching in.

More hands made the work load light.
To get the job done they worked day and night.

They realized the joy they found in this town
and were glad they decided to stick around.

When they got down to the last bit of soil,
you wouldn't believe it...the family Struck Oil!

They jumped and shouted with all their might.
They hit it big and life changed overnight.

What a valuable lesson they learned
    that day,
that sometimes life's little blessings
come in the most mysterious way.

Who would have thought the Hill family
would go from Ashes to Black Gold?
This is the grandest story ever told!

JULIE'S SPECIAL RECIPE
#14 Creative Vision

Months have passed since the county fair
where Julie, Joe, and Oliver's ice cream flavor
won with no compare.

The townspeople continued to ask day after day
for them to create new flavors to send their way.

Since Julie loved making things that were sweet,
she thought, "Why not, this could be such a treat."

Her eyes got bigger as her vision became clear,
"I can start an Ice Cream Business later this year!"

She thought of the wonderful flavors she could create
and how the townspeople would line up at her gate.

Idea after idea came into her head
as her imagination was fed.

"New flavors fashioned after Grandma's recipes
that could be my very own specialty."

Julie couldn't wait to call Oliver and tell him the news.
She picked up the phone and started to dial
and got more excited as they chatted a while.

After hearing her ideas, Oliver readily agreed
a Summer Ice Cream Business would surely succeed.

Too bad Joe couldn't participate.
He spent summers away with his Great Uncle Nate.

Although the trio was now down to two
this was a task this pair could do.

Off to work Julie and Oliver began
creatively making a business plan.

The sky was the limit they couldn't deny
the townspeople would gladly buy buy buy!

Julie jotted down recipes she learned long ago.
Sweet treats like Blueberry Muffin Cookie Dough
and Chewy Cherry Pie in a big Donut Hole...

Triple Chocolate Fudge with Whip Cream on top.
With all these amazing flavors no one would stop
eating more ice cream day after day
and sending more townspeople their way.

And with so many spectacular flavors to choose
their imagination grew and their business did too.
Making Julie's Creative Vision a dream come true!

HAPPY TEETH
#15 Maintenance of Sound Health

Oliver enjoyed all of his tasty ice cream treats,
day and night he would eat eat eat.

Until one day his tooth felt very sore,
it was something he could not ignore.

He dreamt the dentist pulled all his teeth out
so he woke up in a sweat and began to shout!

Oliver ran into his big brother's room,
hoping to be saved from his certain doom.

"I don't want to lose my teeth
from all the sweets stuck underneath."

Big Zeke half asleep laughed in Oliver's face,
"Stop being a baby. It's not as bad as you think.
Not all of your teeth will end up in Dr. Green's sink."

"I really wish you would stop waking me up,
you are worse than Cody, our pup."

Oliver regretted not brushing his teeth
as well as he knew he should
and would do it differently if he could.

Around the breakfast table that morning
as the family ate bacon, eggs, and toast,
Oliver could only eat jello at most.

His mother sensing that something wasn't right,
asked Oliver why he hadn't taken a bite.

Finally Oliver decided to come clean
even though he didn't want to go see Dr. Green.

"Mom, I've been in so much pain,
my teeth are driving me insane.
But I'm scared to get them all pulled out,
please help me before I scream and shout!"

"Oh dear, I'm sure it won't be that bad,
we'll go see the dentist, trust me you'll be glad."

To Dr. Green's office they went and he was redeemed.
It wasn't anything like Oliver had dreamed.
All he needed was to get his teeth cleaned.

Not brushing his teeth was something he couldn't hide.
The soreness was caused by the sprinkles stuck inside.

He said he'd learned his lesson that day,
on the importance of brushing the proper way.

Oliver burst into his new *Happy Teeth Song*
and he encourages you to now sing along:

"It's fun to brush my teeth each and every day,
brushing up and down keeps cavities away.
Two minutes in the morning and two minutes at night,
brushing them daily keeps them nice and bright.
Now my teeth are happy and yours can be too.
I'm glad Dr. Green showed us what to do!"

PAY YOURSELF FIRST
#16 Budgeting Time & Money

Big Zeke was looking up at the sky
as planes raced and flew really high.

In an instant they would flip upside down
and loop and loop and loop all around.

Big Zeke and his dad enjoyed the High Flyer Show.
They were so glad they decided to go.

After the High Flyer Show came to an end,
into the gift shop Big Zeke went to spend spend spend.

He picked up everything from model planes
to goggles, even t-shirts and a pen!
Paying no attention to cost,
his shopping had no end.

Once his arms were overflowing with things to buy,
he walked up to the register and stepped aside.
Looking to his dad to buy it all, but his dad replied,
"Nice try! Where's your money to buy all of this, Son,
you get a weekly allowance and now you have none???"

Big Zeke said, "I have no idea where my money goes.
As soon as I get a dollar in my hand
it slips through my fingers like grains of sand.
I can't help but spend it, isn't that what you do?"

"No, Son. There is a lesson I want to share with you,
a lesson that will last your whole life through.
Big Zeke this is something I wish I learned as a child,"
said Dad, wrapping his arm around him as he smiled.

"You never want to spend more money than you earn.
Pay Yourself First, is the lesson you must learn."

"Set aside at least 10% or more if you can.
Here son, let me help you to understand.
Out of every single dollar you make,
listen carefully, Son, ten cents is yours to take
and put aside to save and grow for you."

"At first glance this may seem like a small amount
but over time it can become humongous and count.
You'll be able to do whatever you want to do
including buying model planes, even real ones too!"

Big Zeke got excited and began to understand
that saving his money was the perfect plan.

He decided today was the best day to start.
Paying himself first would play a big part
in helping him get the money he would need
to bring about his wildest dreams indeed.

His dad allowed him to pick one item from the bunch
that he'd treat him to along with his favorite lunch.
Big Zeke picked the model plane he saw in the show
as a symbol of how he would make his money grow.

Big Zeke hugged his dad with all of his might,
as he knew his future would be very, very bright!

LIVING OUT LOUD
#17 Cosmic HabitForce/Universal Law

Big Zeke stumbled upon a secret door
well hidden in the family's basement floor.
He ran to his room with the contents
    in hand
telling Oliver and Olivia to meet him
    as planned.

"I found these two envelopes covered in dust
which said only open around those you trust."
Oliver ready to see what Big Zeke found
sat quietly next to Olivia on the ground.

He opened the envelope labelled *Penalties You Pay.*
It listed bad habits you must avoid each day:
*"Being lazy and stubborn and drifting through life
ungrateful and jealous and full of much strife."*

*"These are things that will bring lots of pain.
Avoid these as you'll have nothing to gain."*

Olivia chimed in, "I don't like that list!
I want a life filled with happiness and bliss."
Big Zeke and Oliver readily agreed,
"Let's open the other envelope and read."

The second envelope labelled *Rewards You Gain*
contained a list that wouldn't cause pain:
"Decide what you want and follow through,
have faith and courage and love what you do.
Just as the sun goes up it must come down.
What you give you get, it all comes back around.
The riches of life will be yours to take
and the life you live is yours to make."

Big Zeke and Oliver stared off into space
and Olivia sat quietly trying to embrace,
the words they read certainly gave them a chill.
It was signed, *"All the best to you,* Grandpa Hill."

"I think I finally got it," Oliver said with pride.
"The more good I do, the more happiness I keep.
When I form good habits, it's rewards that I'll reap!"

Big Zeke and Olivia said,
    "Yes, that's it!
Living that way we'll be happier,
    you must admit.
Let's get started today and make
    Grandpa proud
by forming good habits and living
    out loud!!!"

Conclusion

We hope you enjoyed coming along for the ride
and allowing Olivia, Big Zeke and I be your guide.
Now it's your turn to learn from these lessons too,
as situations arise you'll know exactly what to do.
Please be sure to keep this amazing book close to you.
If you want to make your wildest dreams come true,
reading from it daily will give you a clear view.
Make sure you stay in touch, there's so much more to do.
Life is full of amazing adventures and success that awaits you!

Your Friend,
Oliver

About the Authors

Prior to becoming certified, each leader certification candidate is required to complete a project related to the 17 Success Principles that are the basis of the curriculum for certification. The project must be done voluntarily as a "give-back" to the Foundation without compensation. Diane and Havilah's combined project is the treasury of children's rhymed stories that incorporate the 17 Success Principles as an introduction to the Science of Success for early readers.

Havilah Malone is an Author and Speaker from New Orleans who graduated from college at the age of nineteen with a degree in Arts & Communications and a minor in Psychology. Havilah is also a youth advocate and founder of the non-profit foundation *Living Beyond the Box, Inc.* The foundation's premiere program, *Everybody Loves Barbie,* fosters a self-empowerment movement that helps youth break the silence of abuse and develop the courage and confidence to live life on their own terms. Havilah is the  youngest of four brothers and sisters and attributes much of her success to the Napoleon Hill principles she learned as a youth. She is a Certified Instructor for the Napoleon Hill Foundation.

Diane Lampe is President and COO of The Lampe Company, LLC, a financial services business she owns and operates with her husband, Bill. Diane has used Napoleon Hill's master work, *The Law of Success,* in building the business for the past 10 years. She attributes much of their success to understanding and teaching Napoleon Hill's 17 Principles of Success. As a mother and recent grandmother, she has spent years in raising their children to believe that the path to success is through applying these success  principles. Now, she is working toward taking Hill's principles to the next generation. She is a Certified Instructor for the Napoleon Hill Foundation.

#1 Definiteness of Purpose

Finding the thing you love to do or what is most important to you and spending your time and energy focused on doing it the very best you can. Having a purpose and a plan is the starting point of all success. Once you learn how to use the power of your mind, you begin to keep your mind on the things you want and off the things you do not want and success will be yours!

#2 Mastermind Alliance

When two or more people work together to achieve a goal. Each person in the group works hard, and is friendly and supports the other members of the group. Everyone in the group benefits from the efforts of the group whether financially or in others ways.

#3 Applied Faith

Using the power of your belief to get a good outcome and taking action towards the outcome to show that your belief is real.

#4 Going the Extra Mile

Doing more than you are expected to do without expecting something in return. And in time all of your extra effort will bring you very big rewards in one form or another.

#5 Pleasing Personality

Being the very best YOU, as only you can be. Your personality is the combination of your behavior, attitudes and traits that make you, "you." It can determine whether people like or dislike you.

#6 Personal Initiative

Making an extra effort to do the things you should do without being asked to do them. Taking charge of your own actions and being a self-starter. Personal initiative is the twin principle of Going the Extra Mile.

#7 Positive Mental Attitude

Keeping your mind on the things you want and off of the things you don't want. Even if things are not going the way you want them to at the time, finding the good in the situation. Making the choice to be happy and in a positive state of mind no matter what is happening.

#8 Enthusiasm

The feeling that you have when you really want something or are very excited. It's an intense emotion that comes from inside of you and can be felt by others around you. It can be seen in the joyful way you approach your day or the things you are doing.

#9 Self-Discipline

Self-control that comes from taking responsibility for your thoughts and actions and making the choice to do what is right. Knowing when to do something or when not to do something and taking the appropriate action.

#10 Accurate Thinking

Understanding why things are done in a certain way so that you can understand how it helps you become better. Not jumping to conclusions or just following popular opinion. Gathering the facts in order to make an informed decision based on knowledge and/or experience about any matter that is presented to you.

#11 Controlled Attention

Paying close attention and concentrating on what you want to learn. Keeping your mind focused on what you want to accomplish leads to mastery in any given area of life.

#12 Teamwork

Working together to accomplish a goal that everyone wants. Your teammates can be friends, family, volunteers or anyone who is freely willing to help out.

#13 Learning from Adversity and Defeat

No matter what happens in life, even when it is bad, there is some benefit that can come from the situation. You must search for the good. Even when you feel defeated, it is not a failure unless you accept it as such. You don't have to lose, you can always consider it learning.

#14 Creative Vision

Using your imagination to dream bigger and break through any limitations so that new ideas flow through your mind. You learn and apply new ways of doing things. Then take those ideas and write them down so that you can create a plan of action to make them a reality.

#15 Maintenance of Sound Health

Keeping your mind and body healthy by forming good habits. Being active and caring for it by eating well, being clean and getting proper rest. Your mind must be fed positive thoughts, reading and viewing material because your thoughts help create your experience of life and affects the overall health of your body.

#16 Budgeting Time and Money

There are twenty-four hours in a day and how you spend your time is very important. To accomplish your goals you must pay close attention to what you do during the day so that you will not waste either time or money. Money is a tool that can help you accomplish your goals and it must be used wisely and put to work for you.

#17 Cosmic Habitforce

The process of how the universe works in an orderly manner. When you engage in an activity or behavior on a regular basis it becomes a habit, you no longer have to think about it, you are able to do it automatically. You see this daily in nature, the entire process works on a regular schedule. Whatever seeds are planted is what will bloom.

List of Suggested Children's Books by Principle

Principle #1 - DEFINITENESS OF PURPOSE

1. *What is My Song?* Written by Dennis Linn, Sheila Fabricant Linn, & Matthew Linn SJ. Paulist Press. 2005.
2. *Follow the Moon.* Written by Sarah Weeks. Illustrated by Suzanne Duranceau. HarperCollins Publishers. New York. 1995.
3. *The Tale of Three Trees.* Retold by Angela Elwell Hunt. Illustrated by Tim Jonke. Kingsway Communications. England. 1989.

Principle #2 - THE MASTERMIND ALLIANCE

4. *Stone Soup.* Jon J. Muth. Scholastic Press. 2003.
5. *The Little Red Hen.* The Talking Mother Goose Series. Retold by Margaret Huges. Worlds of Wonder. 1986.
6. *The Classic Treasury of Aesop's Fables.* Illustrated by Don Daly. Running Press. 1999. Pg. 47.

Principle #3 - APPLIED FAITH

7. *The Trellis and the Seed.* Jan Karon. Penguin. 2003.
8. *Leo the Late Bloomer.* Robert Kraus. Pictures by Jose Aruego. Windmill Books. New York. 1971.
9. *The Velveteen Rabbit.* Written by Margery Williams. Illustrated by Don Daily. Courage Books. Philadelphia, PA. 1997.

Principle #4 - GOING THE EXTRA MILE

10. *The Dandelion Seed.* Written by Joseph Anthony. Illustrated by Cris Arbo. Dawn Publications. Nevada City, California. 1997.
11. *The Giving Tree.* Written and illustrated by Shel Silverstein. HarperCollins Publishers. New York. 1992.
12. *The Carrot Seed.* Written by Ruth Krauss. Illustrated by Crockett Johnson. HarperCollins Publishers. New York. 1973.

Principle #5 - PLEASING PERSONALITY

13. *Buttons.* Written by Tom Robinson and illustrated by Peggy Bacon. Penguin. New York. 1991.
14. *The Jolly Postman* by Janet and Allan Ahlberg. Tien Wah Press. Malaysia. 2001.
15. *Pete the Sheep-Sheep* by Jackie French and illustrated by Bruce Whatley. Clarion Books. New York. 2004.

Principle #6 - PERSONAL INITIATIVE

16. *Brother Wolf of Gubbio.* Written and illustrated by Colony Elliott Santangelo. Handprint Books. New York. 2000.
17. *Jam & Jelly* by Holly and Nellie. Written by Gloria Whelan. Illustrated by Gijsbert van Frankenhuyzen. Sleeping Bear Press. Chelsea, Michigan. 2002.
18. *Angelina Ballerina.* Katharine Holabird. Illustrated by Helen Craig. Pleasant Company Publications. Middleton, Wisconsin. 2000.

Principle #7 - POSITIVE MENTAL ATTITUDE

19. *The Little Engine That Could!* Retold by Watty Piper. Illustrated by George & Doris

Hauman. Platt & Munk Publishers. New York. 1976.

20. *The Frog Prince* by Brothers Grimm. Grimm's Fairy Tales. Diversion Books. New York. 2015.

21. *Aladdin & The Magic Lamp.* Written by John Patience. Once Upon a Storytime Series. 1988.

Principle #8 - ENTHUSIASM

22. *How I Became a Pirate.* Written by Melinda Long. Illustrated by David Shannon. Harcourt, Inc. Mexico. 2003.

23. *The Secret Remedy Book: A Story of Comfort and Love.* Karin Cates and Wendy Anderson Halperin. Orchard Books. 2003.

24. *Granddad's Fishing Buddy.* Written by Mary Quigley. Illustrated by Stephane Jorisch. Penguin. New York. 2007.

Principle #9 - SELF-DISCIPLINE

25. *The Quilt Maker's Gift.* Written by Jeff Brumbeau. Illustrated by Gail de Marcken. Scholastic Press. New York. 2001.

26. *Daniel O'Rourke: An Irish Tale.* Written by Gerald McDermott. Puffin Books. Penguin. New York. 1986.

27. *The Dance.* Written by Richard Paul Evans. Illustrated by Jonathan Linton. Simon and Schuster. New York. 1999.

Principle #10 - ACCURATE THINKING

28. *Seven Blind Mice.* Written by Ed Young. Philomel Books. New York, New York. 1992.

29. *The Fisherman & His Wife.* Written by The Brothers Grimm. Illustrated by John Howe. 1983.

30. *The True Story of the Three Little Pigs!* Written by John Scieszka. Illustrated by Lane Smith. Puffin Books. Penguin. New York. 1989.

Principle #11 - CONTROLLED ATTENTION

31. *The Three Questions.* Written and illustrated by Jon J. Muth. Scholastic Press. New York. 2002.

32. *A Small Child's Book of Prayers.* Collected and Illustrated by Cyndy Szekeres. Scholastic Press. New York. 2002.

33. *The Itsy Bitsy Spider.* Told and illustrated by Iza Trapani. Whispering Coyote Press. Dallas, Texas. 1993.

Principle #12 - TEAMWORK

34. *Together...We can.* Written by Beth Shoshan and Petra Brown. Paragon. United Kingdom. 2012.

35. *Don Quixote and Sancho Panza.* Adapted by Margaret Hodges. Illustrated by Stephen Marchesi. Charles Scribner's Sons Books for Young Readers. New York. 1992.

36. *Meet the Orchestra.* Written by Ann Hayes. Illustrated by Karmen Thompson. Harcourt. New York. 1991.

Principle #13 - LEARNING FROM ADVERSITY & DEFEAT

37. *Tear Soup.* Written by Pat Schwiebert and Chuck DeKlyen. Illustrated by Taylor Bills.

Grief Watch. Portland, Oregon. 2004.

38. *I'm Sorry.* Sam McBratney. Illustrations by Jennifer Eachus. HarperCollins Publishers Ltd. 2000.

39. *Alexander and the Terrible, Horrible, No Good, Very Bad Day.* Written by Judith Viorst. Illustrated by Ray Cruz. Aladdin Paperbacks. Division of Simon and Schuster. 1972.

Principle #14 - CREATIVE VISION

40. *What Do You Do With An Idea?* Written by Kobi Yamada. Illustrated by Mae Besom. Compendium, Inc. Seattle, WA. 2013.

41. *Roxaboxen.* Written by Alice McLerran. Illustrated by Barbara Cooney. Lothrop, Lee & Shepard Books. New York. 1991.

42. *Where The Wild Things Are.* Written and illustrated by Maurice Sendak. Harper Collins. 1991.

Principle #15 - MAINTENANCE OF SOUND HEALTH

43. *Waiting for Benjamin.* A Story about Autism. Written by Alexandra Jessup Altman. Illustrated by Susan Keeter. Albert Whitman & Company. Illinois. 2008.

44. *Me, Stressed Out?* Written and illustrated by Charles Schulz. Harper Collins. 1996.

45. *What's Happening to Grandpa?* Written by Maria Shriver. Illustrated by Sandra Speidel. Little, Brown and Company and Warner Books. New York. 2004.

Principle #16 - BUDGETING TIME & MONEY

46. *The Busy Beaver.* Written and illustrated by Nicholas Oldland. Kids Can Press, Ltd. Ontario, Canada. 2011.

47. *No Room for Napoleon.* Written by Adria Meserve. Random House. New York. 2006.

48. *What Time Is It, Mr. Crocodile?* Written by Judy Sierra. Illustrated by Doug Cushman. Harcourt, Inc. New York. 2004.

Principle #17 - COSMIC HABITFORCE

49. *All I See Is Part Of Me.* Written by Chara M. Curtis. Illustrated by Cynthia Aldrich. Illumination Arts. Washington. 1994.

50. *Old Turtle.* Written by Douglas Wood. Watercolors by Cheng-Khee Chee. Scholastic Press. New York. 1992.

51. *Sofia's Dream.* Written by Land Wilson. Illustrated by Sue Cornelison. Little Pickle Press LLC. California. 2010.

52. *Winnie the Pooh.* Written by A. A. Milne. Penguin Group. New York. 2009.

For additional information about Napoleon Hill products please contact the following locations:

Napoleon Hill World Learning Center
Purdue University Calumet
2300 173rd Street
Hammond, IN 46323-2094

Judith Williamson, Director
Uriel "Chino" Martinez, Assistant/Graphic Designer
Alan Chen, Technical Assistant

Telephone: 219-989-3173 or 219-989-3166
email: nhf@purduecal.edu

Napoleon Hill Foundation
University of Virginia–Wise
College Relations Apt. C
1 College Avenue
Wise, VA 24293

Don Green, Executive Director
Annedia Sturgill, Executive Assistant

Telephone: 276-328-6700
email: napoleonhill@uvawise.edu

Website: www.naphill.org